DATE DUE

NOV 0 2 2011		
MAY 2 5 2012		

CLOSE-UP

INSECTS

BROWN
BEAR
BOOKS

Published by Brown Bear Books Limited

An imprint of
The Brown Reference Group plc
68 Topstone Road
Redding
Connecticut
06896
USA
www.brownreference.com

ISBN: 978-1-93383-414-6

Authors: John Woodward and Leon Gray
Designer: Lynne Lennon
Picture Researcher: Rupert Palmer
Managing Editor: Bridget Giles
Production Director: Alastair Gourlay
Children's Publisher: Anne O'Daly

Picture credits
Front cover: Science Photo Library: David Scharf
Title page: Science Photo Library; Andrew Syred
Science Photo Library: Georg Bernard 25, Biophoto Associates 29, Dr. Jeremy Burgess 11, 23, 27, Susumu Nishinaga 13, Claude Nuridsany & Marie Perennou 5, 7, David Scharf 19, 21, Andrew Syred 9, 15 , 17.

Library of Congress Cataloging-in-Publication Data

Insects.

    p. cm. – (Close-up)

  Includes bibliographical references and index.

  ISBN-13: 978-1-933834-14-6 (alk. paper)

  1. Insects–Juvenile literature.

QL467.2 .I5826 2007

 595.7 22

2006103052

Printed in China
9 8 7 6 5 4 3 2 1

Contents

On the Wing   4

Colorful Scales   6

Fly Feet   8

Compound Eyes   10

Sense of Smell   12

Aphid Appetites   14

Winged Ones   16

Insect Vampires   18

Liquid Diet   20

Caterpillar Change   22

Aphid Explosion   24

Ant Colonies   26

Woeful Weevil   28

Glossary   30

Further Study   31

Index   32

On the Wing

An adult insect beats its wings to fly. The wings are fixed to the top of the insect's body. They are made from a flat sheet of chitin. Hard rods called veins run through the wings. The veins make the wings stiff. The hard layer that covers the insect's body is also made from chitin. It protects the insect's soft insides.

Flying Tuning Fork

Some small flies beat their wings more than 1,000 times a second. The smaller the insect, the faster it beats its wings. The sound an insect makes as it flies comes from the moving wings. If a tiny insect beats its wings 440 times a second, the sound is the same as that of the musical note A.

Inside or out?

Most flying animals use muscles inside their wings to fly. Insects do not have muscles inside their wings. They beat their wings and fly using muscles inside the body. Some insects can fly for hours before the muscles tire.

This dragonfly's wing is criss-crossed with hard rods called veins. The veins carry air, blood, and nerves through the wing. They also support the wing.

Colorful Scales

The wings of most butterflies and moths are covered with tiny scales. Some of the scales are round and flat. Others look like tiny hairs. The wings are made from a tough material called chitin.

Shiny scales

The wings of many butterflies and moths are bright and colorful. Some of the color is on the scales. Some of it comes from light bouncing off the scales. The bouncing light makes the wings look shiny. Some moths have no wing scales. Their wings are clear and have no color.

Becoming Bald

If you touch the wings of a butterfly or moth, your fingers will become covered in shiny scales. A butterfly or moth can lose so many scales that its wings lose their color and no longer work.

Colorful scales form an eyespot on the wing of this Spanish moon moth. The moth flashes its eyespot when it is in danger. The eyespot scares away the attacker.

Fly Feet

Like all insects, a fly has six legs. The foot at the end of each leg has two curved claws. The claws help the fly hold onto bumpy surfaces. Each foot also has two soft pads that press down onto smooth surfaces. The foot pads produce a sticky liquid that acts like glue.

Safety Stripes

Many flies have yellow and black stripes around their bodies. They look like the warning stripes of the stinging bees and wasps. The stripes on the flies trick insect-eating animals such as birds. The birds think the flies can sting like bees and wasps. The birds leave the flies alone.

Walking up walls

How does a fly walk up a wall? The two claws on each foot grip onto bumps on the wall. The pads stick to the wall. As the fly walks, it unpeels the pads on three feet. The pads on the other three feet stay stuck to the wall. This stops the fly from falling off the wall.

Compound Eyes

Our eyes help us see the things around us. A large lens inside each eye gathers light. Our brain uses the light signals to build up a picture of our surroundings. An insect's eye works in the same way. But it is made up of thousands of tiny lenses.

Building images

Each lens in an insect's eye sends light signals to the brain. The brain builds up a picture of dots from each lens. More lenses in the eye means more dots in the picture. A dragonfly can have 30,000 lenses in each eye!

An Insect's View

Use a magnifying glass to look at the picture of the fly's eye on the opposite page. You will see that the picture is made up of many tiny dots. An insect probably sees things as patterns of dots.

A fly's eye is called a compound eye. It has thousands of lenses. Each lens sends light signals to the fly's brain. The brain forms a picture the fly can see.

Sense of Smell

Many insects have a good sense of smell. At night, a moth uses smell to find food. The moth feeds on sweet-smelling nectar inside flowers. The moth smells the nectar using two long, feathery antennae on the top of its head. Male moths also use their sense of smell to find female moths.

After Dark

The flowers of some plants have a stronger smell at night. An example is honeysuckle. Moths smell the strong nectar and fly to the flowers to feed. As they feed, they carry tiny grains of pollen from one plant to another. Plants use pollen to make seeds, which grow into new plants.

Special smell

Females send out a special smell called a pheromone. The feathery antennae of a male can pick up the smell of the female's pheromone from more than a mile away. The male moth follows the smell of the pheromone to find his mate.

Tiny hairs cover the antennae of a moth. The hairs are the moth's "nose." They help the moth smell food and find other moths in the dark.

Aphid Appetites

Aphids feed on the sap from plants. They poke their sharp, tubelike mouthparts into a plant and suck up the sap. Other insects feed in the same way. For example, mosquitoes suck up the blood of people and animals using their sharp mouthparts.

Sugary sap

Plant sap is full of sugar but has little protein. Aphids need protein to grow, so they must drink a lot of sap. As a result, they eat much more sugar than they need. They get rid of the extra sugar as a sticky, syrupy liquid called honeydew.

Honeydew Herds

Many types of ants love honeydew. An ant will lick up the sugary liquid as it comes out of the aphid's body. Some ants sometimes keep "herds" of aphids so they can feed on the honeydew. The ants protect the aphids from attackers.

Winged Ones

Most flying insects have two pairs of wings. For some flying insects, the rear wings and front wings move separately from each other. Dragonflies are an example. For other flying insects, such as bees and butterflies, the two pairs of wings link up and move as one. A few types of flies have only one pair of wings.

Ancient Insects

Scientists have found the remains of insects that lived millions of years ago. The remains are locked away inside rocks in the ground. From these remains, scientists know that giant dragonflies lived more than 300 million years ago. Their wings measured more than 2 feet (60 cm) across.

Linking up

The paired wings of flying insects link up in different ways. When a butterfly flies, its front wings push down on its back wings. In bees and wasps, rows of tiny hooks hold the front and back wings together.

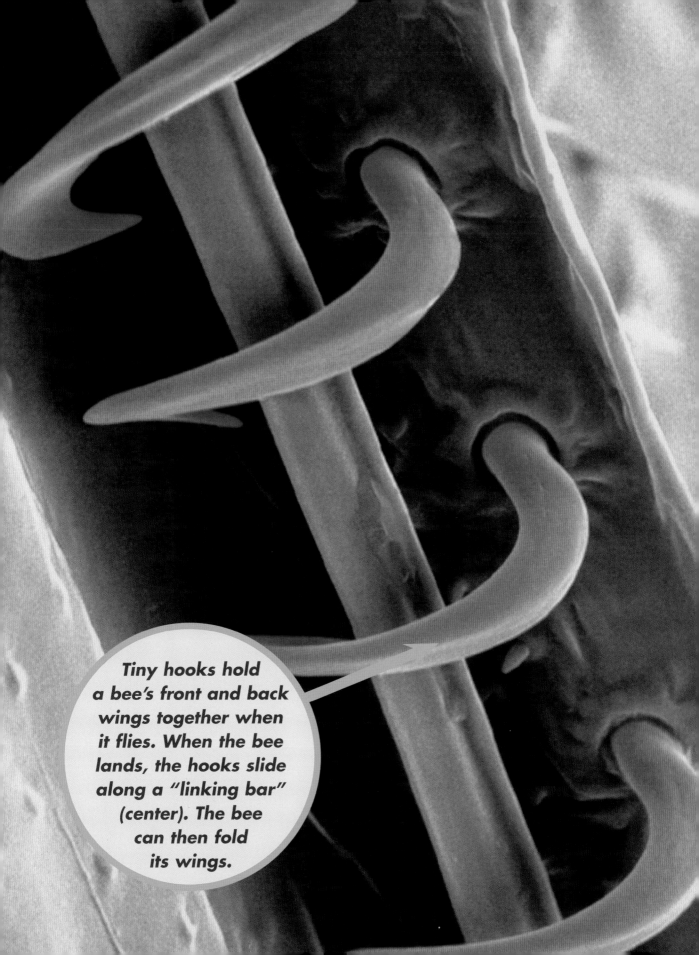

Tiny hooks hold a bee's front and back wings together when it flies. When the bee lands, the hooks slide along a "linking bar" (center). The bee can then fold its wings.

Insect Vampires

Mosquitoes feed by sucking up liquids through a long, hollow tube called a stylet. Male mosquitoes feed on sugary plant sap. Females need a meal of human blood before they can lay their eggs.

Bloodsuckers

A female mosquito pokes her sharp, needlelike stylet through a person's skin. The blood then rushes up the hollow tube and fills the mosquito's stomach. The female injects a special chemical into the blood to keep it flowing. This chemical makes a mosquito bite sore and itchy.

Tropical Invaders

Some mosquitoes that live in hot, humid countries carry tiny creatures inside their bodies. These creatures cause dangerous diseases such as malaria and yellow fever. They enter the body when the female mosquito feeds on a person's blood.

The body of this African yellow fever mosquito is swollen with human blood. You can see the long, hollow stylet poking out from the mosquito's head.

Liquid Diet

Some insects feed on plants or other animals. Other insects cannot eat solid food. They look for liquid food. The liquid must contain all the energy the insects need to stay alive. Tiny insects called fruit flies cannot eat solid food. Instead, they feed on the juices of rotting fruit.

Colossal Chromosomes

Chromosomes occur inside the center of animal and plant cells. Chromosomes contain instructions to make new cells. One fruit fly has enormous chromosomes. Scientists use this fruit fly to figure out how cells use their chromosomes to make new cells.

Finding the food

A tiny bruise or broken skin on a piece of fruit is a perfect meal for a fruit fly. Fruit flies find their food using their sense of smell. The antennae on their head track down the smelly rotten fruit. The fly then sucks up the juices using its tubelike mouthparts.

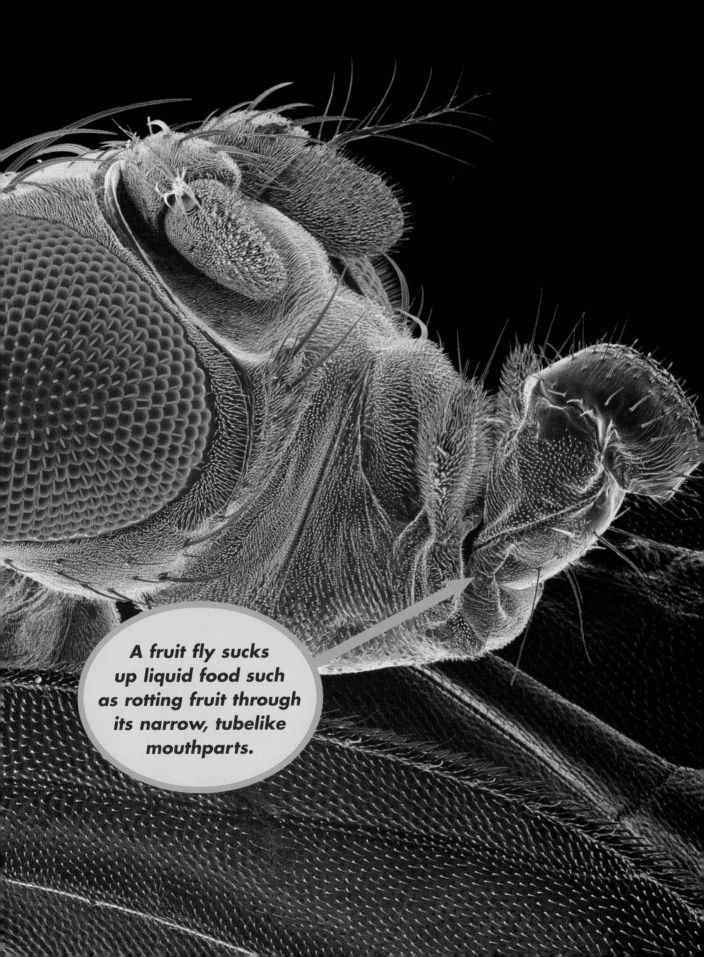

A fruit fly sucks up liquid food such as rotting fruit through its narrow, tubelike mouthparts.

Caterpillar Change

Many insects start life in one body form. The insects then change completely into another body form. For example, a butterfly starts life as an egg that hatches as a caterpillar.

Cycle of life

A caterpillar spends most of its time eating leaves. When it is ready, the caterpillar surrounds itself in a shell called a pupa. Inside the pupa, the caterpillar changes into a butterfly. The butterfly then breaks out from the pupa. Males and females mate. The females then lay eggs that hatch as new caterpillars.

Brief Glory

Many butterflies do not eat. They live on the energy stored when they were caterpillars. The main reason for the butterfly stage is to find a mate and lay eggs. Once this is done, the butterfly dies.

A caterpillar hatches by eating its way through the egg case. Young caterpillars eat leaves and grow quickly before they change into butterflies.

Aphid Explosion

In the fall, male and female aphids mate. The females lay eggs. The eggs hatch as female aphids in the spring. Over the summer, the female aphids produce young without mating with males. Some females bear four or five young every day. All the young aphids are females like their mother.

Danger, Danger!

An aphid faces many dangers. For example, attackers such as ladybugs and lacewings eat aphids. When the aphid meets an attacker, its body makes a tiny drop of a chemical called "alarm pheromone." The chemical warns other aphids in time for them to make their escape.

Peak population

The young females are soon ready to have their own babies. Within a few weeks, there is a huge number of aphids. Finally, a few males are born in the fall. These males and females mate and produce new eggs.

A female aphid gives birth to a young female. This young aphid has no father. It will grow into an exact copy of its mother.

Ant Colonies

Ants live in groups called colonies. A "queen" ant rules the colony. She lays all the eggs that hatch and grow into new ants. The other ants serve the queen and her young. These ants are called workers. They hunt food and look after the nest.

Ant attack

The strong jaws of some ants are deadly weapons. The Australian bulldog ant uses its painful bite to defend its nest and kill animals for food. Other ants spray harmful chemicals at their enemies.

Ant Antics

Some ants keep other ants as slaves. The ants often steal slaves from a nearby colony when they are young. Army ants live in hot, humid (wet) forests. These ants march through the forest. They kill and eat every animal in their path, including birds and small mammals.

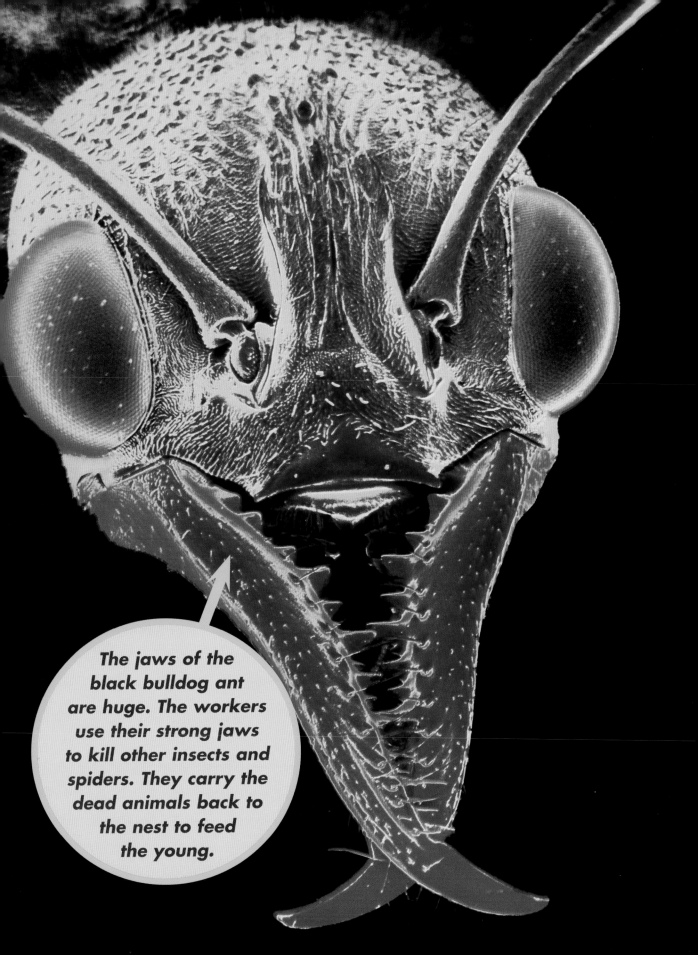

The jaws of the black bulldog ant are huge. The workers use their strong jaws to kill other insects and spiders. They carry the dead animals back to the nest to feed the young.

Woeful Weevil

Many insects are pests. They destroy plants that farmers grow as food for people. One pest is the grain weevil. The grain weevil has strong jaws. It chews through the tough outer covering, or husk, of grains such as wheat. It feeds on the rich food inside the husk.

Ship's Biscuits

Centuries ago, sailors used to eat ship's biscuits during long trips at sea. Ship's biscuits were a simple mix of flour, salt, and water. While they did not hold much food value, the biscuits could be stored for months at sea. The biscuits were also food for weevils. So sailors often ate the weevils as part of their biscuit food.

Life cycle

Female weevils lay their eggs inside grains. The young hatch as grubs. The grubs feed on the food inside the grain. When they have eaten all the grain, the grubs change into adult weevils. Females lay eggs inside new grains. The life cycle is complete.

A tiny weevil feeds inside a single grain of wheat until it becomes an adult. The adult chews through the grain. It leaves the empty shell, or husk, behind.

Glossary

antennae: the "feelers" on top of an insect's head; they are used for touching and smelling.

cells: tiny building blocks that make up the bodies of all living creatures.

chemical: any substance found in nature or made by people.

chitin: the tough substance that hardens the body and wings of insects.

chromosomes: tiny "threads" in the cells of living creatures that contain the instructions for life.

disease: something that stops the body of a living creature from working properly.

lens: the clear, curved structure that focuses light inside the eye.

pest: an unwanted insect that destroys food, crops or livestock.

pheromone: a chemical produced by one animal to attract other animals of its kind.

pollen: small, yellow grains that are the male parts of a flower.

pupa: a stage in an insect's life when it turns from a grub into an adult.

sap: the watery liquid inside a plant.

stylet: long, tubelike mouthpart of some insects.

Further Study

Books

Blobaum, Cindy. *Insectigations: 40 Hands-on Activities to Explore the Insect World.* Chicago: Chicago Review Press, 2005.

Dell, Pamela. *Do Bed Bugs Bite?: A Book About Insects.* Mankato, Minnesota: First Facts Books, 2007.

Insect (Eye Know). New York: DK Publishing, 2006.

Weber, Rebecca. *Tricky Insects: And Other Fun Creatures.* Mankato, Minnesota: Compass Point Books, 2006.

Wimmer, Theresa. *My First Look At: Insects* (various titles). Pittsburgh, Pennsylvania: Creative Education, 2006.

Web sites

projects.edtech.sandi.net/encanto/insectsK
Find out how insects look, what they eat, where they live, and their special features with this kindergarten site.

www.enchantedlearning.com/themes/insects.shtml
The Enchanted Learning web site features hundreds of fun activities, crafts, and games to help you learn about the wonderful world of insects.

Index

antennae 12, 13, 20
ants 14, 26–27
 army ant 26
 bulldog ant 26, 27
 workers 26
aphids 14, 24–25

bees 8, 16, 17
birds 26
blood 5, 14, 18, 19
brain 10, 11
butterflies 6, 16, 20, 22, 23

caterpillars 22, 23
cells 20
chitin, 4, 6
chromosomes 20

dragonflies 10, 16

eggs 18, 22, 23, 24, 25, 26, 28
eyes 10–11
eyespots 7

flies 8–9, 11, 16
 fruit flies 20, 21
foot pads 8, 9
fruit 20, 21

hairs 6, 8, 13
honeydew 14

jaws 26, 27, 28

lacewings 24
ladybugs 24
lenses 10, 11

malaria 18
mammals 26
mosquitoes 14, 18
moths 6, 12
mouthparts 14, 15, 20, 21
muscles 4

nectar 12

pests 28
pheromones 12, 24
plants 12, 14, 15, 18, 20, 28
pollen 12
protein 14, 15
pupae 22

sap 14, 15, 18
scales 6
ship's biscuits 28
spiders 27
stylet 18, 19

warning stripes 8
wasps 8
weevils 28–29
wings, 4, 5, 6, 16, 17
 wing hooks 16, 17

yellow fever 18